ASTROLOGY

A Guide to Eastern and Western Horoscopes

Astrology

A Guide to Eastern and Western Horoscopes

Sasha Fenton

Barnes
& Noble
BOOKS
NEW YORK

Contents

Introduction
How To Use This Book

This book gives an overview of many different *astrology*[1] traditions, and then shows you your personal character profile in each of them. If you want to know what your month of birth means not only in Western astrology but also in Chinese, Vedic, Native American, Celtic or Norse Runic astrology, here is your opportunity to find out.

The first part of this book tells you about a host of ancient and modern types of astrology.

The middle section of the book contains a monthly calendar for the various signs. To find the signs that apply to you, select the month in which you were born. Look at the first day of the month. This shows which signs were in operation in all the systems on the first day of each month, so if you happened to have been born on the first of the month, all these will be yours. If you were born on any other day, you will have to track through the calendar to see when each different type of astrology sign changed and therefore which apply to you. You might like to have a pen and paper handy for this.

For example, if you were born on 25 January, this would be your picture:

Western astrology:	Aquarius
Chinese astrology:	Receptive Earth, Ox
Vedic astrology:	Makara, like Capricorn
Mansion 25:	Purva Bhadra
Native American astrology:	Otter, Butterfly clan
West African astrology:	The Baobab Tree
Celtic Tree astrology:	Cypress
Norse Runic astrology:	Pertho

Once you have listed all your signs, read through the interpretations in the latter part of this book to see what they tell you about your character.

[1] All items in *italics* appear in the Glossary. Note that italics are used only the first time the term appears in this book.

HISTORY AND BACKGROUND

The roots of all astrology systems grew out of the need to fix a calendar for agriculture; the agricultural 'year' itself then became punctuated by religious festivals. These festivals mark turning points of the year – the right time to start planting or to move animals to higher or lower pastures, for instance. Europe, the Middle East and the Indian subcontinent all developed systems that originated in what is now Iraq. Western astrology moved from Iraq to Egypt, then on to the ancient Greeks and Romans. Chinese astrology started in the areas around the Yellow River. Central American astrology originated with the Maya and Toltec people, and was developed further by the Aztecs; some of this permeated North American Indian astrology, although local myths and local observation of the sky also play a part in the Native American tradition. African astrology developed from Egyptian and north African studies of animal marks on sandy or soft soils, in addition to studying the heavens. Norse and Celtic astrology are an amalgam of pagan myths and measurements of the sun's movement.

Ancient people believed that planetary movements signalled events such as floods, good and bad harvests or wars with neighbouring tribes, and so the predictive aspects of astrology soon followed. Early astrologers believed that the position of the planets rising over the horizon or at the top of the sky at a person's birth foretold the potential character and destiny of that person. This kind of thinking was never applied to common people – it was only used for royal babies and the sons of military, the priesthood or court leaders.

The popularization of astrology in our own age came about through just this kind of royal *horoscope*. In 1930, a British astrologer outlined and interpreted a chart for the infant Princess Margaret for an article in a national newspaper. This article was so popular that the editor asked the astrologer if he could do something for the general public. He did. From this point, newspaper astrology took off. The original article also sparked interest in more detailed forms of astrology.

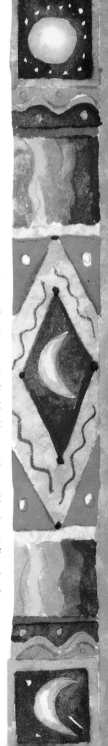

About Western Astrology

The Basics

If you can put yourself into the minds of those who lived before the solar system was discovered, it is easy to see why they believed that the sun travels around the Earth rather than the other way around. This *apparent* pathway of the sun around the Earth is called the *ecliptic*. The constellations of stars that lie along the ecliptic are the signs of the *zodiac* we are familiar with – from Aries to Pisces. (The signs run in this order because the tropical zodiac starts at the spring equinox in the northern hemisphere – on 21 March. This becomes the start of the sign of Aries; the rest of the signs follow from Taurus to Pisces.) The moon and the planets also travel close to this path, although they cross up and down over it from time to time. For the sake of simplicity, astrologers call everything a planet, including the sun and the moon. Planets are at various angles to one another, depending upon where they are along this line – astrologers call these angles *aspects*. If, for instance, Venus was on one side of the Earth while Saturn was around the other side, this would be described as an opposition between Venus and Saturn.

Astrologers work from charts that show the position of the planets, the aspects and many other important features. A natal or birth chart is set for a specific date, time and place of a person's birth, and it is in actual fact a stylized illustration of the sky at the moment of a person's birth. Such a chart can also apply to the birth of a country, a city, a business, a marriage or any other kind of enterprise. By plotting the movement of the planets against the natal chart, we can predict the trends and events that unfold over a period of time.

The familiar kind of astrology that we see every day in newspapers and magazines is called sun sign astrology. The Earth has a regular orbit around

8

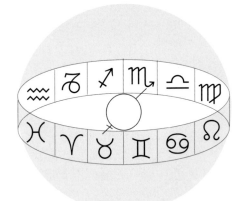

♈	Aries	♋	Cancer	♎	Libra	♑	Capricorn
♉	Taurus	♌	Leo	♏	Scorpio	♒	Aquarius
♊	Gemini	♍	Virgo	♐	Sagittarius	♓	Pisces

the sun, and this makes the sun appear against the background of each sign of the zodiac in turn at set times of the year. This makes it easy for non-astrologers to work out which sign they are born under. Unfortunately, the sun enters each sign at a different time and sometimes even on a different day from one year to the next, which means that people born 'on the cusp' (the point where one sign joins another sign) can find themselves described as belonging to either the ending or the beginning sign by different news-papers or magazines. Astrologers use the exact degree for each individual, but newspapers have to use an average date, and they don't all settle on the same one. If you are not absolutely sure which sun sign you come under, a quick check with an astrologer will soon tell you.

YOUR SUN SIGN

The sun itself is a life-giving force, and its position on your horoscope is bound to influence your personality, affecting your potential for success, creativity and happiness in various areas of life. The sun on a horoscope is

often associated with creativity, talent and chances of success in business, in entertainment, and in having a good time. It is also concerned with the children in your family. The sun shows how you choose to spend your time and your money, and what you most enjoy. Your sun-sign nature is modified by other features on your birthchart, but it is usually apparent somewhere, and you will always have similarities with those who share your sun sign.

YOUR RISING SIGN

Your *rising sign* (also called your *ascendant*) is the sign that was crossing the eastern horizon when you were born. It is determined by the time of day, plus the date, plus the place where you were born. It tells you about the influences that were around you during your childhood, and it modifies your sun sign considerably. The sign opposite your rising sign is called your *descendant,* and affects your choice of friends, lovers, colleagues, and partners.

THE MOON AND THE PLANETS

The moon's position at your birth is almost as important as your sun sign. The moon rules the emotional side of your nature, and its place in your birthchart reveals your underlying nature and motives. It is wise to check the *elements* and *qualities* of the moon sign of any person with whom you are likely to become deeply involved, as these may show you parts of that person that are quite different from what is being displayed on the outside.

Each planet rules a different aspect of a person's nature and of life – for example, a potentially flighty person can be anchored by Mars and Venus in earth signs, or a stodgy one can be lightened by Mercury, Venus, Mars or Jupiter in air or fire signs. Fire signs show enthusiasm and impetuosity, earth signs denote practicality, air signs belong to ideas people, while water signs are intuitive and emotional. Astrologers study many other features on a horoscope, both for character reading and also for prediction. These might include the *midheaven*, the descendant, the *nadir*, the asteroids, *midpoints*, fixed stars, the *vertex* and much more, depending upon the skill of the astrologer and the nature of the work he or she wishes to do.

PREDICTION

There are a number of predictive techniques in astrology, but they all come down to checking the position of the planets at a specific time against their positions on the natal chart, to see what is happening and what is due to happen over a particular period of time.

GEORGE W BUSH
(known affectionately as 'Dubya')
6 July, 1945
06:26 EST
New Haven,
Connecticut, USA

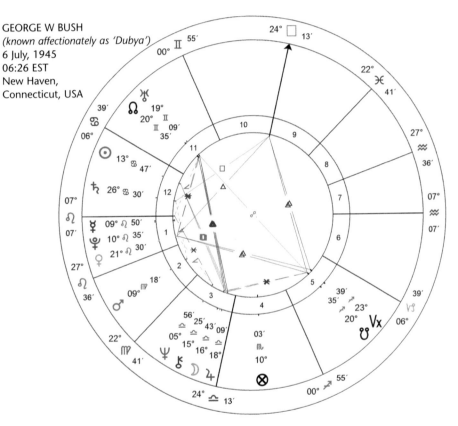

Western: Sun in Cancer, Leo Rising
Chinese: Receptive earth Goat
   (Also Year of the Dog)
Vedic: Mithuna
Mansion 10: Magha

Native American: Woodpecker
   of the Frog clan
West African: The Judge
Celtic tree: Fir
Norse Runic: Fehu
Sun sign astrology

THE WESTERN ZODIAC
THE ZODIAC

The zodiac is the group of constellations that lie along the path that the sun appears to take around the Earth.

THE SYMBOLS

Each sign of the zodiac is associated with a planet and a symbol. Every other sign, (starting with Aries, then Gemini, etc) is *positive,* and the remaining signs are *negative.* Some astrologers express this concept with the words *masculine* and *feminine,* or even *yang* and *yin,* but the meaning is the same. Each sign also belongs to an element and a *quality* that give it a particular character. Your sign of the zodiac will have something in common with several others, but there are always four signs with which you don't share anything. However, you may have other factors in your individual chart not immediately apparent in a general description of your sign of the zodiac. Here are the signs of the zodiac with their basic features so that you can see how this fits.

Aries, Taurus, Gemini, Cancer, Leo, Virgo, Libra, Scorpio, Sagittarius, Capricorn, Aquarius, Pisces

Positive, masculine or yang signs have an extroverted, assertive and quick-thinking nature. These are Aries, Gemini, Leo, Libra, Sagittarius and Aquarius. Negative, feminine or yin signs are introvert, slower to react and more passive in nature. These signs are Taurus, Cancer, Virgo, Scorpio, Capricorn and Pisces.

The positive group splits again into the elements of fire and air. Fire signs are quick, impulsive, enthusiastic and quick to anger, but also quick to cool down. These are Aries, Leo and Sagittarius. The air group is more intellectual, thoughtful and inclined to fuss and worry. These signs are Gemini, Libra and Aquarius.

The negative group splits again into the elements of earth and water. Earth signs are practical, sensible and disinclined to jump into new things. These are Taurus, Virgo and Capricorn. The water group is sensitive and inclined to act from an emotional standpoint. These signs are Cancer, Scorpio and Pisces.

These signs are also grouped according to whether they are cardinal, fixed or mutable. The cardinal signs are go-getters, fixed signs uphold the status quo and mutable signs bring change and closure. The cardinal signs are Aries, Cancer, Libra and Capricorn. The fixed signs are Taurus, Leo, Scorpio and Aquarius, and the mutable signs are Gemini, Virgo, Sagittarius and Pisces.

ARIES

21 March to 20 April

SYMBOL: The Ram

RULING PLANET: Mars

GROUPS: Positive, fire element, cardinal quality

Some Arians come across as loud, while others are quiet and reserved; either way you don't allow the grass to grow under your feet. You are competitive both at work and in your hobbies, and you can gain a high position in life through a combination of hard work and adroit political skills. You are keen on art and music but you are unlikely to work in these fields. Passion is your ruler, both in terms of love and sex and also in terms of what you believe to be important. You try hard in marriage and love your children deeply.

TAURUS

21 April to 21 May

SYMBOL: The Bull

RULING PLANET: Venus

GROUPS: Negative, earth, fixed

Yours is the most stable sign of the zodiac – you will stick to jobs and relationships as long as humanly possible. Being reliable, patient, tenacious and conscientious, you are valued as a worker and you excel in any field in which you can use your hands and your creative talents. The other side of this coin is your famous obstinacy. You value a happy partnership more than anything and your home is important to you, so you do all you can to make it attractive and comfortable. You are surprisingly sociable and you make friends easily, but friends are not as important to you as your family. You like saving for a rainy day.

Gemini

21 May to 21 June

Symbol: The Twins
Ruling planet: Mercury
Groups: Positive, air, mutable

You often want two things at once. You need the stability of a happy relationship, a regular job and a settled home, but you also need variety or you soon become bored. You usually find your way into a job that puts you into contact with many people and gives you a variety of different tasks to do during the course of the day. Worrying about relatively unimportant matters is your weakness, and you can get on your own nerves as well as those of others. You like buying good clothes, and you are unlikely to live in untidy or uncomfortable surroundings.

Cancer

22 June to 22 July

Symbol: The Crab
Ruling planet: The moon
Groups: Negative, water, cardinal

Your basic nature is cautious and protective: you don't enjoy taking crazy chances, and you hate the thought of your family being in any kind of trouble. You have a responsible and sensible attitude to your working life, often choosing a job that puts you in touch with the public and which supplies some of their needs. You are slow to fall in love and steadfast once you have done so, because you take all relationships seriously. However, you can be somewhat moody and hard to fathom, especially when you feel hurt or if you are upset by the atmosphere around you. You enjoy travel and novelty, but you also love coming home again.

LEO
23 July to 22 August
SYMBOL: The Lion
RULING PLANET: The Sun
GROUPS: Positive, fire, fixed

Your nature is generous, outgoing, humorous and creative, but your standards can be high, which can make you seem arrogant or dismissive of others. You are an excellent organizer and an energetic entrepreneur, but you also enjoy family life and are deeply attached to your children. At work you are energetic and efficient, but you can become irritated when things don't go your way. In love, you are passionate, but you may have a habit of falling for the wrong type of person until you learn better; when you find the right person, you are steadfast and faithful. You may be the last of the big spenders, but you always earn enough to make up the shortfall.

VIRGO
23 August to 22 September
SYMBOL: The Virgin or Maiden
RULING PLANET: Mercury
GROUPS: Negative, earth, mutable

Clever, conscientious and thorough, you get the job done. Being attuned to mental rather than physical jobs, you love to work with ideas and with words. You are more of a backroom person than a leader, but you need to be appreciated for the hard work you put in. You have few important relationships, but you are intensely loyal to those who matter to you. You prefer to show your love by doing things for your partner rather than by simply being affectionate. Your worst problems are fussiness and a tendency to worry unnecessarily about health. You are usually careful with money, apart from occasional binge spending on books and records.

LIBRA
23 September to 22 October
SYMBOL: The Scales
RULING PLANET: Venus
GROUPS: Positive, air, cardinal

Being ruled by the Scales, it is no wonder that you often see every side of an argument and that you find it difficult to make your mind up. Your charm and ability to handle people make you an excellent agent or arbitrator. At work, you are happiest when among those who encourage you to make the most of your considerable talents. At home, you are best with a protective and loving partner, but you can also enjoy your own company. Your excellent taste means that your appearance and your home are always a la mode. You can spend money freely, but you are quite lucky with finances, so you can usually find a way out of trouble.

SCORPIO
23 October to 21 November
SYMBOL: The Scorpion
RULING PLANET: Pluto
GROUPS: Negative, water, fixed

You have a mixture of characteristics, and there are times when you can switch between personalities. For most of the time, you are reasonable, hard-working, sensible, intelligent, humorous and loving, but you can turn into a critical control freak. You are a hard and reliable worker, but you prefer to be the power behind the throne than to sit on it yourself. You can be quite competitive, which can get you a long way in your career, and if you can channel it into sports or some other activity, you achieve considerable success and enjoy yourself at the same time. You are extremely loyal to those who you love, especially your children, and you always want the best for them.

Sagittarius
22 November to 21 December
Symbol: The Archer
Ruling planet: Jupiter
Groups: Positive, fire, mutable

Most of you are outgoing, generous, humorous and enthusiastic, but not all are like this. You enjoy large projects, and many of you are excellent builders and handypersons. You prefer a skilled type of job that takes you from place to place and in which you meet a number of different people. Being restless, you love to travel, and you may actually end up living in a different country from the one in which you were born. Some of you are quiet and introspective, and you can all confuse a lover by your sudden lapses into silence and your lack of feedback. You adore your family, and take special interest in your children's education, and you are generous and helpful to your partner.

Capricorn
22 December 21 January
Symbol: The Goat
Ruling planet: Saturn
Groups: Negative, earth, cardinal

Some of you are outgoing and happy to be in the limelight, others are shy and retiring, but all of you are ambitious. Your ambitions may be just for yourself, but they are often also for your family, your employers or your country. Being a hard and reliable worker, you are usually respected and appreciated for what you do, but you can be fussy or demanding. In love, you want a total relationship, and to be secure in the knowledge that you come first. When happy in a relationship, you are caring, protective, and very loving. You adore your children and you are a faithful and dependable partner. You enjoy travel, but you love coming home again.

Aquarius
22 January to 20 February
SYMBOL: The Water Carrier
RULING PLANET: Uranus
GROUPS: Positive, air, fixed

Being highly independent, you like doing things your own way, but you can always be swayed by logical argument. You are reasonable, humorous, friendly and trusting, until someone hurts you. Being highly intelligent and fond of gadgets, your inventive mind will take you into the world of new technology or offbeat ideas. At home, you are a loving but possibly careless homemaker, preferring to make intriguing toys for your children than to plump up cushions. You feel that life is too interesting to spend your time worrying about money or practicalities, although you can solve these problems when you have to. You need a partner who understands your quirky ways.

Pisces
21 February to 20 March
SYMBOL: The Fishes
RULING PLANET: Neptune
GROUPS: Negative, water, mutable

You may have two sides to your personality, one side being kind, caring and apt to sacrifice yourself for others. The other side can be surprisingly bossy, but your sensitive nature means that you feel any hurt very deeply and you are quick to understand the feelings of others. You are intuitive and often psychic, with an inner feeling of certainty that there is more out there than meets the eye, and this leads you into a deep interest – and occasionally a career in – spiritual subjects. Your partner must understand your need to pursue your interests as well as your need to leave the house for days at a time when work calls. Your values are spiritual rather than materialistic, so you may never make much money.

Western Rising Signs

During the course of each 24-hour period, the sun rises in one part of the world after another. People with the same birthday share the same sun sign, but they could have any one of the 12 signs rising up over the horizon, depending upon their time and place of birth.

The following method offers a rough guide to your rising sign. Find out what time the sun rises on your birthday, deducting one hour if daylight saving was in effect.

1 Look at the illustration. You will notice that it has the time of day arranged around the outer circle. It looks a bit like a clock face, but it is different because it shows the whole 24-hour day in two-hour blocks.

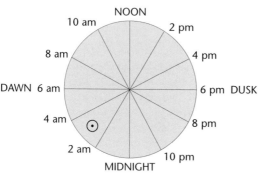

2 Write the astrological symbol that represents the Sun (a circle with a dot in the middle) in the area that corresponds to your time of birth.

3 Now write the name of your sign or the symbol for your sign on the line at the end of the block of time that your Sun falls into. Our example shows a person who was born between 2 am and 4 am under the sign of Pisces.

4 Either write in the names of the zodiac signs or use the symbols in their correct order around the chart in an anti-clockwise direction, starting with your own sign, as shown in the example.

5 The sign that appears on the left-hand side of the wheel at the 'Dawn' line is your rising sign, or ascendant. The example shows a person born with the Sun in Pisces and with Aquarius rising. You will always find the ascendant sign on the 'Dawn' line and the descendant sign on the 'Dusk' line.

20

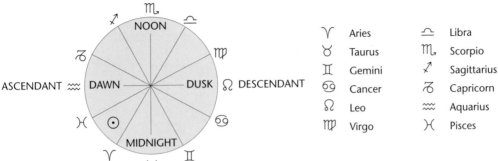

♈	Aries	♎	Libra
♉	Taurus	♏	Scorpio
♊	Gemini	♐	Sagittarius
♋	Cancer	♑	Capricorn
♌	Leo	♒	Aquarius
♍	Virgo	♓	Pisces

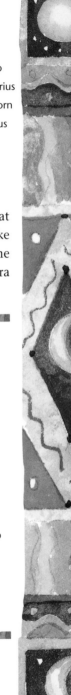

The rising sign relates to your early experiences of life and the things that influenced you in childhood. You may behave -- and even look – more like your rising sign than your sun sign. The following is a brief outline of the effects of the rising signs; the section on your Western sun sign has extra information about the character of the sign that is rising.

Aries rising
Your outer manner is quiet and reserved.

Taurus rising
You have a calm outer manner, but with seething emotions beneath, and you may be possessive.

Gemini rising
You may be friendly and intelligent, but you often feel like an outsider.

Cancer rising
You have a responsible attitude and are good to your family.

Leo rising
You are attracted to glamor and unusual people or careers.

Virgo rising
You are overly self-critical.

Libra rising
You are attractive and charming but can tend towards laziness.

Scorpio rising
You have poor relationships until you find the right lover.

Sagittarius rising
You need freedom and space.

Capricorn rising
You are cautious in love and with money.

Aquarius rising
You are intelligent and tend to be drawn to an unusual lifestyle.

Pisces rising
You are partly practical, businesslike, organized, careful with money, and partly spiritual, mystical, chaotic.

CHINESE ASTROLOGY
THE BACKGROUND

Chinese astrology was originally based on the movement of the seven stars of the Dipper, plus the Pole star and Vega, as well as the cycles of the planets Jupiter and Saturn. Buddhist monks used predictive techniques for the benefit of their followers; however, at one point a series of repressive emperors outlawed astrology. Since they were not allowed to use actual stargazing, the monks found ways of incorporating the horoscope system into a calendar and numerology system that was already in use. The famous animal signs were a Buddhist invention that simplified the preceding system and made it more accessible.

The elements in Chinese astrology are wood, fire, earth, metal and water. Each element has a different character. Wood is idealistic; fire is intellectual and enthusiastic; earth is practical; metal is determined and stubborn; and water is artistic, businesslike and communicative. The names of the signs and elements vary a little from place to place; they also reflect the differences in nationality of those 19th century Europeans who translated the system into their own languages. Here are the main differences:

Rat, Mouse.
Ox, Buffalo.
Rabbit, Cat.
Snake, Serpent.
Goat, Sheep.
Rooster, Cockerel, Hen, Chicken.
Pig, Boar.
Wood, Tree.
Earth, Soil.
Metal, Gold, Iron.

THE FULL SYSTEM

The full Chinese astrology system is called 'The Four Pillars' or 'The Four Emperors.' It incorporates signs, elements, yang and yin, and the I Ching. It relies upon the time, place, day, month and year of birth and it is extremely complex. This system requires the use of a special logbook called the 'Universal or Perpetual Calendar.' It is only available in Chinese and has never been properly translated into English.

The usual procedure is to work out the sign and element for each year, then for each month, for each hour and finally for each day. Most popular Chinese horoscope books concentrate on the annual and hourly systems. However, we will also look at the monthly system, as it isn't difficult to understand, and it fits nicely with the monthly readings later in this book.

THE SIGNS AND ELEMENTS FOR EACH MONTH

The Chinese monthly system starts the year with the month of February, which is around the time of the Chinese New Year. The original system would have run from 4 February, this being the 'imperial' new year's day, with each month starting on the fourth, but modern astrologers usually work from the first of each month.

Each season contains three months. We start with the spring season of February, March and April. Each season contains an element that rules two months in a row; the last month is always ruled by the element of earth. The thinking behind this relates to the fact that each element also refers to a direction –the directions are more commonly used in other divination systems, such as the Feng Shui, the I Ching and the Lo Shu. The directions are water for north, fire for south, wood for east, metal for west, with earth taking us back to the center. Ancient Chinese civilization was confined to the area around the Yangzte and Yellow rivers in northern China, so when traders and imperial emissaries traveled the waterways to distant outposts, they always returned to the civilized Middle Kingdom. This idea of traveling out and then and back to the center again originated then.

THE ANIMALS, ELEMENTS, YANG AND YIN

The animal signs alternate between yang and yin but the elements are neutral, so when an element is attached to an animal sign that is yang, it becomes *active*, and when it is attached to an animal sign that is yin, it becomes *receptive*.

Animal	Energy
Rat	Yang
Ox	Yin
Tiger	Yang
Rabbit	Yin
Dragon	Yang
Snake	Yin
Horse	Yang
Goat	Yin
Monkey	Yang
Rooster	Yin
Dog	Yang
Pig	Yin

The yang, or active energy, rules the masculine or positive characteristics of assertion, drive, ambition, originality and the will to fight. The yin, or receptive energy, rules the feminine or negative characteristics of nurturing, conserving, protecting, enduring and continuing. If you consider warriors or inventors on one hand and farmers and homemakers on the other, you will see how both yang and yin are necessary for humanity to change and progress (yang) and to continue and conserve (yin).

Most Chinese astrology books only offer information on the situation for the year in which you were born; this book concentrates on the monthly picture for all the different forms of astrology. However, if you know your year sign you will find some information on it in the monthly section of this book.

THE SIGNS FOR EACH HOUR

The ancient Chinese broke the day into two-hourly segments, each of which is ruled by one of the animal signs; if you know what time you were born, you can find out which is your hourly sign from the table below. If you were born during daylight saving, you will need to deduct one hour from your time of birth. If you are not sure which of two signs you come under, read both. The interpretations for each of the animal signs are in the monthly sections of this book.

The Hour	The Animal
11pm to 1am	Rat
1am to 3am	Ox
3am to 5am	Tiger
5am to 7am	Rabbit
7am to 9am	Dragon
9am to 11am	Snake
11am to 1pm	Horse
1pm to 3pm	Goat
3pm to 5pm	Monkey
5pm to 7pm	Rooster
7pm to 9pm	Dog
9pm to 11pm	Pig

VEDIC ASTROLOGY
THE SIMILARITIES & DIFFERENCES BETWEEN VEDIC & WESTERN ASTROLOGY

V edic astrology is practiced in India, Sri Lanka and surrounding areas. It takes seven years to gain a degree in Vedic astrology in a good school in India. A knowledgeable Western astrologer can read a basic Vedic chart because the differences are not so great, but beyond the basics, the two systems diverge. Vedic charts are usually square in shape, although some Indian astrologers also use round charts similar to those used in the West.

One glaring difference is that Western astrologers use the tropical zodiac while Vedic astrologers use the sidereal zodiac. The tropical zodiac starts at the spring equinox in the northern hemisphere on 21 March. This becomes the start of the sign of Aries; the rest of the signs follow from Taurus through Pisces. Vedic astrology is based on the constellations rather than the equinoxes,

so it uses sidereal time (star time) rather than Earth or calendar time. The constellations on which Vedic astrology is based have moved since the rules of Western astrology were originally laid down around 2,000 years ago, precessing backwards through the zodiac. In Western astrology prior to the Christian era, the earth was moving through the sign of Taurus, then moved to Aries, which in turn entered the sign of Pisces at the start of the Christian era. We are now on the cusp of the sign of Aquarius. The rules for Vedic astrology, however, were laid down after the time of Christ, which means that if you were born in the Western sign of Libra, by Vedic astrology you would now be a Virgoan. If you construct a Vedic chart for a time several hundred years in the future, your sun sign would shift even further back into Leo.

Vedic astrologers don't concentrate on the signs of the zodiac in the way Western astrologers do. Vedic astrology is far more complicated, taking into account the exact degree of each planet's position in the sky and the many different ways of dividing and interpreting a chart, which is beyond the scope of this book.

Modern Vedic astrology uses all ten planets, though some systems revert to the older form, which only uses the seven planets that people can see with the naked eye. The seven planets are the sun, moon, Mercury, Venus, Mars, Jupiter and Saturn; the later discoveries are Uranus, Neptune and Pluto.

Vedic astrology is frequently used for predictive purposes such as plotting the best time to start an enterprise or the best date for a marriage. One common form of character reading used is that of an astrologer assessing a child's potential for a future career through the details of his or her chart.

I have an Indian friend called Kussum who is a doctor. One day, I casually asked Kussum what had made her choose medicine as a career, expecting her to reply that her parents or older brothers had been doctors, because medicine so often runs in families. She replied that none of her family was a doctor, but that her father had taken her details to an astrologer when she was about seven years old, and the astrologer had suggested medicine as an appropriate career choice for her. It seemed incredible to me that a whole

family (Kussum included) would base a career choice solely on an astrologer's opinion. Kussum then asked me to look at her Western chart to perform the same exercise of selecting a suitable career for her. I could see no other choice but medicine, so I guess Kussum was in the right job!

THE NAKSHATRAS

One major difference between Western and Vedic astrology is the use of a system called Nakshatras. This type of astrology is also called the *Mansions of the Moon*. The Mansions system turns up in some forms of Arabic astrology, in Chinese astrology, and in even some really ancient Romany types of astrology. It predates our type of zodiac astrology by several centuries, though it is no longer used in Western astrology.

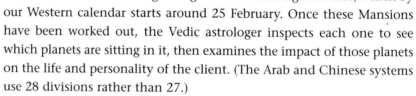

There are 27 Mansions, each one named after a deity or traditional being. Each Mansion is a segment of a circle – a 13° 20′ segment to be exact. The first Mansion starts from the beginning of the sidereal sign of Aries, which by our Western calendar starts around 25 February. Once these Mansions have been worked out, the Vedic astrologer inspects each one to see which planets are sitting in it, then examines the impact of those planets on the life and personality of the client. (The Arab and Chinese systems use 28 divisions rather than 27.)

I have worked out rough dates for these Mansions, putting them in the data section of this book, so you will be able to find the Vedic Mansion for your date of birth in the interpretation section of this book. This is a rather rough guide – if your birthday falls close to the cusp (the point where two signs join) of two Mansions, you should read both. The interpretations that I have given are shamefully brief, but at least they give a flavor of what each Mansion is about. These interpretations have the feel of a previous age about them, and I have not changed that.

Native American Astrology

Native Americans are a diverse group of peoples. The Americas represent a large segment of the world's landmass, and Native Americans have for centuries lived everywhere from the frozen north to as far south as the tropical jungles. Their religious beliefs and practices varied widely. Some started out with a basis in *astronomy* and astrology, while others used *geomancy*, which is the study of landmarks, the marks of animals and other indications on the surface of the land. The earliest forms of star-based astrology systems were Toltec and Mayan; these systems were later taken up by the Aztecs, and in time some of this thinking moved northwards. Nowadays, the mythology and astrology of the North American Indians have crystallized into a popular form of astrology.

Native Americans believe in personal communication with the Creator Spirit, and they receive most of their information through visions, often with the aid of a Medicine Man who is part healer and part clairvoyant. Native Americans also believe in the Earth Mother who looks after the land, and they try to live in harmony with nature. Along the way, a study of the stars became incorporated with these beliefs. Some tribes would view an area of land several miles in diameter as an exact copy of one or more of the constellations.

THE MEDICINE WHEEL

The *Medicine Wheel* is part compass and part wheel of fortune, and it moves through the seasons, through lifetimes and through good times and bad. The full Medicine Wheel is a large, round pictorial almanac that shows the movement of the seasons, planets and constellations during the course of the year. All cultures use wheels and circles to denote the passage of the stars around the Earth, and thus the passage of time, seasons and the events of our lives.

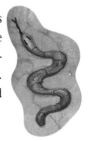

THE MEDICINE WHEEL

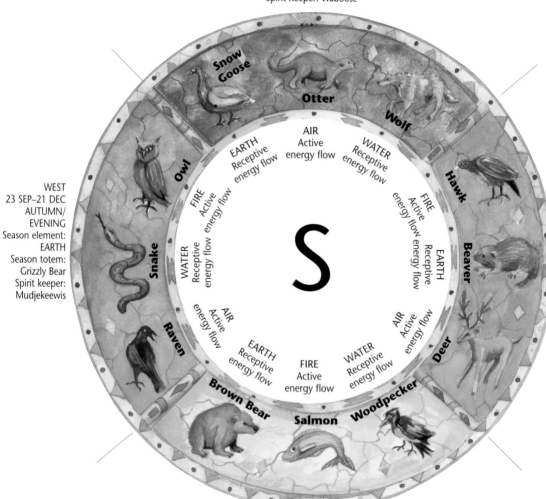

NORTH
22 DEC–20 MAR
WINTER/NIGHT
Season element: AIR
Season totem: White Buffalo
Spirit Keeper: Waboose

WEST
23 SEP–21 DEC
AUTUMN/
EVENING
Season element:
EARTH
Season totem:
Grizzly Bear
Spirit keeper:
Mudjekeewis

EAST
21 MAR–2
SPRING/
MORNING
Season ele
FIRE
Season tot
Eagle
Spirit keep
Wabun

SOUTH
21 JUN–22 SEP
SUMMER/MIDDAY
Season element: WATER
Season totem: Coyote
Spirit keeper: Shawnodese

Note that the S at the center of the Wheel represents the never-ending flow of energy, the life force.

Snow Goose

Otter

Wolf

Owl

Snake

Raven

Brown Bear

Salmon

Woodpecker

Deer

Beaver

Hawk

AIR
Active
energy flow

EARTH
Receptive
energy flow

WATER
Receptive
energy flow

FIRE
Active
energy flow

FIRE
Active
energy flow

WATER
Receptive
energy flow

EARTH
Receptive
energy flow

AIR
Active
energy flow

EARTH
Receptive
energy flow

FIRE
Active
energy flow

WATER
Receptive
energy flow

AIR
Active
energy flow

S

Somewhere along the line, American Indians moved from a lunar calendar to a Western calendar, so their signs of the zodiac now fit reasonably comfortably with our familiar Western ones. One difference is that the cycle starts at the solstice that occurs just before Christmas, rather than the equinox on 21 March.

The American Indians associate each season with a compass point – north is winter, cold and dark, the time when the earth rests. The east brings dawning, awakening and the spring, the south represents the height of summer and the start of the harvest, and the west is the area of strong winds, cooler weather and a time for hunting – or for war. Each season has a Spirit Keeper attached to it.

THE TWELVE SIGNS OF THE NATIVE AMERICAN ZODIAC
Each of the twelve signs of the zodiac also has its own moon, plant, mineral and color. They each also belong to a clan that shares their element – Thunderbird for fire, Turtle for earth, Butterfly for air, and Frog for water.

mal totem	Color	Mineral	Plant	Elemental clan	Northern hemisphere	Southern hemisphere
w goose	White	Quartz	Birch tree	Turtle	12/22–1/19	6/21–7/22
er	Silver	Silver	Aspen	Butterfly	1/20–2/18	7/23–8/22
f	Blue-green	Turquoise	Plantain	Frog	2/19–3/20	8/23–9/22
k	Yellow	Fire Opal	Dandelion	Thunderbird	3/21–4/19	9/23–10/22
ver	Blue	Chrysocolla	Blue lily	Turtle	4/20–5/20	10/23–11/21
r	White & green	Moss agate	Yarrow	Butterfly	5/21–6/20	11/22–12/21
dpecker	Pink	Carnelian	Wild rose	Frog	6/21–7/22	12/22–1/19
non	Red	Garnet & iron	Raspberry	Thunderbird	7/23–8/22	1/20–2/18
wn bear	Purple	Amethyst	Violet	Turtle	8/23–9/22	2/19–3/20
en	Brown	Jasper	Brown	Butterfly	9/23–10/22	3/21–4/19
ke	Orange	Copper	Thistle	Frog	10/23–11/21	4/20–5/20
l	Black	Obsidian	Spruce	Thunderbird	11/22–12/21	5/21–6/20

The Maya & The Aztecs

The Maya developed an early calendar, called the *Solar Calendar*, which contained 18 lunar months, each of 20 days' duration, with an additional five-day month tacked on at the end of the year, for a total of 365 days. According to some, the Mayan calendar predicts that the world is due to come to an end in the year 2012!

The Aztecs conquered the Maya, but they also learned from them, adopting the Mayan Solar Calendar for agriculture. The Aztecs also developed their own calendar, called the Count of the Destinies or the *Destiny Calendar*, which ran for 260 days. It was linked to various astronomical phenomena and used for religious and ritual purposes as well as for divination. Their divination was not the personal kind that we are familiar with; it was used to predict floods, harvests, drought or war with neighboring nations.

The Aztecs believed that the universe was controlled by gods whose powers shifted from one to another in a very delicate balance. This power was either reflected in the stars or kept in place by them, so any change in the cosmos was likely to lead to destruction of the Earth. In the Destiny Calendar, each segment of time was assigned to a god, and rituals were designed to keep these gods happy, the most widely known being the sacrifice of pre-adolescent children.

The Destiny Calendar consists of two continuous sequences, which can be imagined as two interlocking wheels, the first with 13 numbers, the second with 20 symbols. Start the cycle with the number one on the first wheel and the first symbol on the second wheel, with the 13 numbers running in sequence, then starting over, and the 20 signs running in sequence, then starting over. The first number and the first symbol will thus match up every 260 days (13 x 20). The two different Destiny Calendars were used for different purposes, one being religious and the other for general life.

The Solar Calendar rotates in a 52-year cycle vaguely reminiscent of the Chinese system – twelve signs that each rule one year and five elements that rule two years at a time, forming a repeating cycle. When the 260-day Destiny Calendar and the 365-day Solar Calendar start on the same day, it takes roughly 52 years for them to reach their beginning dates on the same day again to start the cycle anew. In the Aztec use of the Solar Calendar, each of the 52 years has a name. There are also 13-year eras that repeat the year names. The first of these is called Calli (one), the second Tochtli (two), and so on. After 52 years (4 times 13), the era name and the year name are the same.

As if this is not confusing enough, each of the twenty symbols in the Destiny Calendar is assigned to a specific god, but some are also assigned to the 13 Destiny Calendar numbers. Remember, we are dealing with a Solar Calendar of 52 years, as well as a Destiny Calendar that comprises two cycles, one with 20 days and another with 13 days. Therefore, one day might be expressed as:

18 Tecpatl Chalchihuitotolin - 9 Atl Xiuhtechuhtli

In this case, the first name represents god number 18 on the Destiny Calendar and day number 9 on the Solar Calendar, but either name could turn up in other places on either calendar.

The Solar Calendar and the Destiny Calendar were eventually taken up by every Central American and Mexican group until the Spanish conquest. The names varied from culture to culture, but the system was the same. The Solar Calendar is still used today in some parts of Mexico. One survivor of the Destiny Calendar is the name of the Aztec god of violent and sudden change, which is Huracan – the root of the word 'hurricane.'

Mayan and Aztec astrology were never used for personal character reading or personal predictions.

CELTIC TREE ASTROLOGY

Trees figured strongly in pagan mythology all over northern Europe, and they were often worshiped, as different types of trees were associated with various ancient gods. The idea of bringing a Christmas tree into the house came to Britain via Queen Victoria's German husband, Prince Albert, providing is a direct link to the earlier pagan beliefs that surround the winter solstice. It is likely that the idea of judging a person's nature and destiny by their type of Celtic tree comes from an ancient system that blended with an early form of solar and lunar astrology.

The Celtic tree system contains 44 signs, each of which has a character of its own. Most signs cover only a few days; the signs for the equinoxes and solstices each have only one day. These one-day signs were attached to pagan rituals that were performed at the turn of each season. There are 23 trees associated with the signs, so some trees rule more than one segment of the year, but differences in temperament are detailed for those born under the same tree signs during different seasons. It would be nice and neat if the Fir tree ruled the Christmas period, but according to Celtic astrology, it is the Apple that rules the winter solstice.

The trees in this system seem to come from all over Europe and the Middle East; it is possible that the system arose in the Celtic areas of northwest Europe and traveled out and then back again, absorbing ideas from other parts of the continent.

Runic Astrology

The Runes are letters of an ancient alphabet; individual letters were traditionally cut into slices of wood or written on smooth pebbles. The Runes originate in northern Europe and Scandinavia. They were devised by people from the Teutonic tribes, and their use spread into the Scandinavian Viking tribes and early Germanic ones such as the Saxons. Tradition has it that the god Odin hung himself upside down from the sacred tree, Yggdrasil. He stayed like this for nine days, during which time he reached enlightenment. At this point, he discovered the Runes lying among the roots of the tree, and he was led to understand their divination meanings and their alphabet.

It is interesting to note that this is the only form of astrology that arises out of the need to devise an alphabet – most of the others arose from the need to develop a usable calendar. Differences arise in the way the names of the Runes are pronounced and spelled depending upon whether the origin of the word is Teutonic, Saxon or Norse/Viking.

The meanings behind the Runes are derived partly from the agriculture, weather, geography and plant life of the people of northern Europe and Scandinavia, and partly from the myths and legends surrounding pagan gods such as Thor, Freya and Odin.

Each Rune sign runs for a period of two weeks. There are 24 Runes in the alphabet, so this fits quite well into an annual system, with the extra four weeks being taken up by the sign of Hagalaz, assigned to the Halloween period, and Jera, which is associated with beginnings and endings, taking Christmas and the period just before the New Year.

Arabic Astrology
The Fortunes

The Arabs developed a form of astrology based on a circular chart and planets in much the same form as Western astrology, but which then takes a completely different approach. This form of astrology is known to Western astrologers as The Arabic Parts and in the Middle East as the *Fortunes of Astrology*. Various Arabic astrologers worked on these Fortunes. In 1029, an astrologer called Al-Biruni compiled a comprehensive list of the24 Fortunes. His book was only updated and properly translated into English in 1980 by an American astrologer called Robert Hurzt Granite.

The starting point for the calculation of each Fortune is the exact degree of the rising sign. This exact degree is known as the ascendant. After this, a series of formulas must be worked through to find each Fortune. One such example is calculated by adding the position of the moon to the position of the ascendant, then calculating the number of degrees between the sun and moon and subtracting this from the first figure.

The formula for the Part of Fortune for a daytime birth:
Ascendant + moon − sun

This formula reverses for night births: the moon's position is subtracted from the ascendant, then the distance between the moon and the sun is calculated and added to the first number.

The formula for the Part of Fortune for a nighttime birth:
Ascendant – moon + sun

The most famous Fortune is the Part of Fortune or Fortuna, which is the only Fortune in common use by Western astrologers. The Part of Fortune shows how a person will make headway in life and whether he or she will gain status or wealth in the world or not. This Fortune is affected by any planet that passes over its position or that makes an angle to it from some other position along the path of the zodiac. Such a planetary movement can have a beneficial effect on a person's fortunes or a devastating one, depending upon the planet in question and the angle it makes.

Calculations for other Fortunes are even more complicated, as they involve the ascendant, two planets and the cusp of a particular astrological house. Some formulas are the same for day and night, others are not. This kind of astrology requires a top-notch astrologer who can either handle the calculations with ease or who has software that can do the job.

There are many of these Fortunes or Arabic Parts, with names such as the Part of Goods, the Part of Brethren, the Part of Servants, the Part of Passion, the Part of Water Journeys, the Part of Imprisonment, the Part of Deception and so on. Together, these Fortunes provide guidance on every aspect of Arabic life.

Ancient Egypt & Ancient Israel

Ancient Egyptian Astrology

Many different forms of astrology were developed in Ancient Egypt, all predating our zodiac and rising sign system. One of the earliest was linked to the movement of the moon – this lives on in an adapted form in Arabic astrology and Vedic astrology as the Mansions of the Moon. One slight difference between the two systems is that the Vedic uses 27 lunar signs while the Arabic uses 28. Later forms of Egyptian astrology were far more like the Western zodiac system.

The Thebaic Calendar

Another system is the Thebaic Calendar. This calendar was used in the city of Thebes when the city was at the height of its power. The Thebaic system divides the ecliptic into 90 divisions, of four degrees each. Each of these had a little illustration or hieroglyph, and each had its own meaning.

Hebrew Astrology

Hebrew astrology assigns letters of the Hebrew alphabet to each sign of the zodiac as well as to each planet. The number of letters in the alphabet varies a little depending upon which tradition is used, but 19 will cover the basics, neatly fitting the twelve signs and the seven planets visible to the naked eye. These letters were mainly used in Hebrew numerology, which like Chinese astrology, might have had its origins in the stars, planets and constellations, but evolved over the years to become far more attached to numbers and their meanings.

West African Astrology

North Africa incorporates Egyptian and Arab cultures, and much of the periphery of the continent has long been infiltrated by other races as traders, colonists, slavers or imported workers. In these areas, writing and record keeping do exist – usually by means of Arabic script. Africans who live in the countryside still study the sky for weather patterns, inspiration and divinatory purposes, but the lack of a written language in the center and south of the continent has held its people back from real scientific study and record keeping.

West Africa has a tradition of geomancy similar to that used in ancient Egyptian sand reading. The Shaman, or wise man, chooses a patch of ground at the approach to the village and outlines this with sticks in a form that resembles a miniature airstrip. Pieces of string are threaded across the strip very close to the ground and in a criss-cross pattern, and then this is left overnight. The following morning the wise man inspects the area and studies the tracks made by animals walking over it during the night.

The original ancient Egyptian method eventually became formalized and incorporated into zodiac astrology. A form of this was later discovered by that great collector of occult knowledge, Napoleon Bonaparte, and it became known as the Oracle of Napoleon. The designs used in the Egyptian method and those of the West African astrology system are very similar.

How to Discover What You Are

You may be aware of your sign of the zodiac in Western astrology, but you won't necessarily know which sign you come under in all the other types of astrology that you will find in this book. It would be nice if all these different divinations lined up so that a Virgo would automatically be a Brown Bear, a Traveler, and a Lime tree, but this is not how it works. Different forms of astrology use different rules: for instance, there are 12 signs in the Western zodiac but 27 Mansions of the Moon in the Vedic system. Even those that do use a 12-sign system all change from one sign to the next on different days of the month.

I have taken two steps to help overcome this problem. The first is the calendar that you will find on the following pages. It gives the starting dates of all the different types of astrology signs. This shows the days on which each of the signs changes, which will enable you to pinpoint exactly which sign you come under in all eight systems. As you will see, it is not enough just to find the correct month of your birth but also the exact day.

The second step is the last section in the book. This gives a character reading for all eight of the signs that are included in each month of the year. In each two-page spread we look at one month, with the second part of one sign of the Western zodiac on the first page and the first part of the next sign on the facing page. Check what the picture is for your actual date of birth. For example, if you were born in the bit of the sign of Aquarius that occurs in January, you will have to look at the month of January, but if you are a February Aquarian you will need to turn over the page.

Unfortunately, the sources of ancient wisdom don't always agree as to the dates when each sign changes. Many of the systems are lunar, which means that they also may not line up exactly from one year to the next. The answer, for those of you who find yourself on the cusp of any sign in any type of astrology, is to read both the signs that are close to your birthday.

January

1							

WESTERN
Capricorn

CHINESE
Receptive
Earth Ox

VEDIC
Dhanus
Like
Sagittarius

MANSION 24
Shatabhishak

NATIVE AMERICAN
Snow Goose
Turtle Clan

WEST AFRICAN
The Harvest
& the
Granary

CELTIC TREE
Apple

NORSE RUNIC
Eihwaz

2	3	4	5	6	7

CELTIC TREE
Fir

WEST AFRICAN
The Baobob Tree

8	9	10	11	12	13

CELTIC TREE
Elm

NORSE RUNIC
Pertho

14	15	16	17	18	19

MANSION 25
Purva Bhadara

NATIVE AMERICAN
Otter
Butterfly Clan

20	21	22	23	24	25

WESTERN
Aquarius

VEDIC
Makara
Like Capricorn

CELTIC TREE
Cypress

26	27	28	29	30	31

MANSION 26
Uttara Bhadra

NORSE RUNIC
Algiz

FEBRUARY

1

WESTERN	CHINESE	VEDIC	MANSION 26	NATIVE AMERICAN	WEST AFRICAN	CELTIC TREE	NORSE RUNIC
Aquarius	Active Wood Tiger	Makara Like Capricorn	Uttara Bhadra	Otter Butterfly Clan	The Baobab Tree	Cypress	Algiz

2 | **3** | **4** | **5** | **6** | **7**

4
WEST AFRICAN
The Wealth of Amber & Silver
CELTIC TREE
Poplar

8 | **9** | **10** | **11** | **12** | **13**

9
CELTIC TREE
Cedar

10
MANSION 27
Revati

12
NORSE RUNIC
Sowelo

14 | **15** | **16** | **17** | **18** | **19**

19
NATIVE AMERICAN
Cougar Frog Clan
CELTIC TREE
Pine
WESTERN
Pisces

20 | **21** | **22** | **23** | **24** | **25**

24
VEDIC
Kumbha Like Aquarius
MANSION 1
Ashwini

26 | **27** | **28** | **29**

27
NORSE RUNIC
Tiwaz

MARCH

1

WESTERN	CHINESE	VEDIC	MANSION 1	NATIVE AMERICAN	WEST AFRICAN	CELTIC TREE	NORSE RUNIC
Pisces	Receptive Wood Rabbit	Kumbha Like Aquarius	Ashwini	Cougar Frog Clan	The Wealth of Amber & Silver	Willow	Tiwaz

2   3   4   5   6   7

5
WEST AFRICAN
The family

8   9   10   11   12   13

9
MANSION 2
Bharani

11
CELTIC TREE
Lime

14   15   16   17   18   19

14
NORSE RUNIC
Berkana

20   21   22   23   24   25

21
NATIVE AMERICAN
Red Hawk Thunderbird Clan

CELTIC TREE
Oak

WESTERN
Aries

22
MANSION 3
Krittika

CELTIC TREE
Hazel

26   27   28   29   30   31

26
VEDIC
Meena Like Pisces

30
NORSE RUNIC
Ehwaz

APRIL

1							
WESTERN Aries	**CHINESE** Active Earth Dragon	**VEDIC** Meena Like Pisces	**MANSION 3** Krittika	**NATIVE AMERICAN** Red Hawk Thunderbird Clan	**WEST AFRICAN** The Family	**CELTIC TREE** Mountain Ash	**NORSE RUNIC** Ehwaz

2	3	4	5	6	7
			MANSION 4 Rohini **WEST AFRICAN** Small Services to the Neighborhood		

8	9	10	11	12	13
			CELTIC TREE Maple		

14	15	16	17	18	19
NORSE RUNIC Mannaz				**MANSION 5** Mrigashira	

20	21	22	23	24	25
NATIVE AMERICAN Beaver Turtle Clan	**WESTERN** Taurus **CELTIC TREE** Walnut				**VEDIC** Mesha Like Aries

26	27	28	29	30
			NORSE RUNIC Laguz	

MAY

1							
WESTERN	**CHINESE**	**VEDIC**	**MANSION 6**	**NATIVE AMERICAN**	**WEST AFRICAN**	**CELTIC TREE**	**NORSE RUNIC**
Taurus	Receptive Fire Snake	Mesha Like Aries	Ardra	Beaver Turtle Clan	Small Services to the Neighborhood	Poplar	Laguz

2	3	4	5	6	7
			WEST AFRICAN The Market		

8	9	10	11	12	13

14	15	16	17	18	19
NORSE RUNIC Inguz	**CELTIC TREE** Sweet Chestnut	**MANSION 7** Punarvasu			

20	21	22	23	24	25
	NATIVE AMERICAN Deer Butterfly Clan	**WESTERN** Gemini			**CELTIC TREE** Mountain Ash

26	27	28	29	30	31
VEDIC Vrishaba Like Taurus		**MANSION 8** Pushya	**NORSE RUNIC** Othila		

JUNE

1

WESTERN	CHINESE	VEDIC	MANSION 8	NATIVE AMERICAN	WEST AFRICAN	CELTIC TREE	NORSE RUNIC
Gemini	Active Fire Horse	Vrishaba Like Taurus	Pushya	Deer Butterfly Clan	The Market	Ash	Othila

2	3	4	5	6	7
		WEST AFRICAN The Ancestor **CELTIC TREE** Hornbeam			

8	9	10	11	12	13
				MANSION 9 Ashlesha	

14	15	16	17	18	19
CELTIC TREE Fig **NORSE RUNIC** Dagaz					

20	21	22	23	24	25
	Native American Woodpecker Frog Clan	**WESTERN** Cancer		**CELTIC TREE** Birch	**CELTIC TREE** Apple

26	27	28	29	30
VEDIC Mithuna Like Gemini	**MANSION 10** Magha		**NORSE RUNIC** Fehu	

JULY

	WESTERN	CHINESE	VEDIC	MANSION 10	NATIVE AMERICAN	WEST AFRICAN	CELTIC TREE	NORSE RUNIC
1	Cancer	Receptive Earth Goat	Mithuna Like Gemini	Magha	Woodpecker Frog Clan	The Ancestor	Apple	Fehu

2 **3** **4** **5** **6** **7**

5 — **WEST AFRICAN** The Judge **CELTIC TREE** Fir

8 **9** **10** **11** **12** **13**

10 — **MANSION 10** Purva Phagune

14 **15** **16** **17** **18** **19**

14 — **NORSE RUNIC** Uruz

15 — **CELTIC TREE** Elm

20 **21** **22** **23** **24** **25**

21 — **NATIVE AMERICAN** Salmon Thunderbird Clan

23 — **WESTERN** Leo

24 — **MANSION 12** Uttara Phalguni

26 **27** **28** **29** **30** **31**

26 — **CELTIC TREE** Cypress

28 — **VEDIC** Karkarta Like Cancer

29 — **NORSE RUNIC** Thurisaz

AUGUST

1

WESTERN	CHINESE	VEDIC	MANSION 12	NATIVE AMERICAN	WEST AFRICAN	CELTIC TREE	NORSE RUNIC
Leo	Active Metal Monkey	Karkarta Like Cancer	Uttara Phalguni	Salmon Thunderbird Clan	The Judge	Cypress	Thurisaz

2	3	4	5	6	7
			WEST AFRICAN The Kola Nut **CELTIC TREE** Poplar		**MANSION 13** Hasta

8	9	10	11	12	13
		MANSION 10 Purva Phagune			

14	15	16	17	18	19
CELTIC TREE Cedar **NORSE RUNIC** Ansuz					

20	21	22	23	24	25
	MANSION 14 Chitra		**NATIVE AMERICAN** Brown Bear Turtle Clan	**WESTERN** Virgo **CELTIC TREE** Pine	

26	27	28	29	30	31
		VEDIC Simha Like Leo	**NORSE RUNIC** Raidho		

September

1

WESTERN	CHINESE	VEDIC	MANSION 14	NATIVE AMERICAN	WEST AFRICAN	CELTIC TREE	NORSE RUNIC
Virgo	Receptive Metal Rooster	Simha Like Leo	Chitra	Brown Bear Turtle Clan	Kola Nut	Pine	Raidho

2 3 4 5 6 7

3
MANSION 15
Swati
CELTIC TREE
Willow

4
WEST AFRICAN
The Traveller

8 9 10 11 12 13

13
CELTIC TREE
Lime
NORSE RUNIC
Kaunaz

14 15 16 17 18 19

20 21 22 23 24 25

21
MANSION 16
Vashaka

23
NATIVE AMERICAN
Raven
Butterfly Clan

23
CELTIC TREE
Olive
WESTERN
Libra

24
CELTIC TREE
Hazel

26 27 28 29 30

28
VEDIC
Kanya
Like Virgo
NORSE RUNIC
Gebo

OCTOBER

1							
WESTERN	**CHINESE**	**VEDIC**	**MANSION 17**	**NATIVE AMERICAN**	**WEST AFRICAN**	**CELTIC TREE**	**NORSE RUNIC**
Libra	Active Earth Dog	Kanya Like Virgo	Anuradha	Raven Butterfly Clan	The Traveller	Hazel	Gebo

2	3	4	5	6	7
		WEST AFRICAN The Distance **CELTIC TREE** Mountain Ash			

8	9	10	11	12	13
					NORSE RUNIC Wunjo

14	15	16	17	18	19
MANSION 18 Chitra **CELTIC TREE** Maple					

20	21	22	23	24	25
			CELTIC TREE Walnut	**WESTERN** Scorpio **NATIVE AMERICAN** Serpent Frog Clan	

26	27	28	29	30	31
		VEDIC Thulaa Like Libra **NORSE RUNIC** Hagalaz			

November

WESTERN	**CHINESE**	**VEDIC**	**MANSION 18**	**NATIVE AMERICAN**	**WEST AFRICAN**	**CELTIC TREE**	**NORSE RUNIC**
Scorpio	Receptive Water Pig	Thula Like Libra	Jyestha	Serpent Frog Clan	The Distance	Walnut	Hagalaz

1

2

3
MANSION 19
Mula
CELTIC TREE
Yew

4
WEST AFRICAN
The Child of the World

5

6

7

8

9

10
MANSION 20
Purvashada

11

12
CELTIC TREE
Chesnut

13
NORSE RUNIC
Nauthiz

14

15

16

17

18

19

20

21

22
NATIVE AMERICAN
Elk
Thunderbird Clan
CELTIC TREE
Mountain Ash

23
WESTERN
Sagittarius
MANSION 21
Urrarashada

24

25

26

27
VEDIC
Vrishchika
Like Scorpio

28
NORSE RUNIC
Isa

29

30

December

1

WESTERN	CHINESE	VEDIC	MANSION 21	NATIVE AMERICAN	WEST AFRICAN	CELTIC TREE	NORSE RUNIC
Sagittarius	Active Water Rat	Vrishchika Like Scorpio	Uttarshada	Elk Thunderbird Clan	The Child of the World	Ash	Isa

2 · 3 · 4 · 5 · 6 · 7

2 CELTIC TREE — Hornbeam

4 WEST AFRICAN — The Harvest & the Granary

7 MANSION 22 — Shravana

8 · 9 · 10 · 11 · 12 · 13

12 CELTIC TREE — Fig

13 NORSE RUNIC — Jera

14 · 15 · 16 · 17 · 18 · 19

17 MANSION 23 — Dhanishta

20 · 21 · 22 · 23 · 24 · 25

22 NATIVE AMERICAN — Snow Goose Turtle Clan

22 CELTIC TREE — Beech

22 WESTERN — Capricorn

23 CELTIC TREE — Apple

26 · 27 · 28 · 29 · 30 · 31

27 VEDIC — Dhanus Like Sagittarius

28 NORSE RUNIC — Eiwaz

YOUR
ASTROLOGY
~
Month
By
Month

January ~ Capricorn
From the 1st to the 19th

The earth sign of Capricorn makes you practical, sensible, ambitious and good to your family. You are less cautious and more interested in art and literature than the December Capricorns. Your Chinese Ox sign makes you a home-lover with a need for comfort and the good things of life. You are practical and thorough, and you work hard because you fear poverty. The receptive earth element ensures that you are capable and efficient, but with an eye for what looks good and what works. Earth people in both these traditions can work with their hands or build a business.

The Vedic sign of Dhanus shows a love of travel and a touch of glamor; your mind is broad and you love to teach and to learn. Your Vedic Mansions are Shatabhishak, which denotes intuition and psychic ability (but it doesn't make for an easy life) and Purva Bhadra, which means you are headstrong and able to cope with hardship. You are a lover of books and poetry.

The Native American Snow Goose of the Turtle clan signifies a traditional outlook and a regal air, and that you are a hard worker with a love of family life. This changes to the inventive, eccentric Otter on the last day of Capricorn. The West African sign of the Harvest and the Granary makes you careful to store up what you need for a rainy day. This combination indicates belief in yourself and self-reliance.

The Celtic Fir suggests a strong-minded but vulnerable personality, the Apple indicates a stylish, refined and sensual nature that is also self-reliant. Elm Capricorns are a little distant with new people. The Norse Runic sign of Eihwaz makes you a stickler for detail but also far-sighted and protective.

January ~ Aquarius
From the 20th onward

The air sign of Aquarius makes you independent and self-reliant, with a keen intellect and an interest in a wide range of topics. The Chinese Ox sign adds much-needed practicality and a hard-working element, while the receptive earth element gives you a keen eye for what looks good and the ability to find ingenious answers to difficult projects.

The adventurous Vedic sign of Dhanus rules the first day of your sign, but the rest belongs to Makara, which gives you a practical and hard-working streak with more ambition and desire for success than outsiders might suspect. Purva Bhadra Mansion makes you a lover of literature and poetry, but also headstrong and sometimes unrealistic. Your karma leads to some areas of suffering in your life. The Mansion of Uttara Bhadra gives you an excellent mind and good speaking abilities in addition to courage, fighting spirit and the ability to shoulder responsibilities.

The Native American Otter of the Butterfly clan makes you clever, bold, playful and helpful, and it gives you a delightful sense of humor and a clear and logical mind. The Baobab Tree of West Africa endows you with authority, honesty, humanity and a realistic attitude.

The Celtic Elm can make you a little distant and detached; the Cypress ensures that you are independent, a little special and rather attractive to look at, but with a somewhat haughty demeanor. You need others to be as straightforward as you are. The Norse Runic sign of Pertho makes it hard for you to understand yourself at times – and occasionally you will be a complete mystery to others – while those Aquarians born under Algiz are even more dreamy! However, you can put your mind, hands and skills to almost anything when the need arises.

FEBRUARY ~ AQUARIUS
From the 1st to the 18th

This second segment of the air sign of Aquarius suggests a talent for arbitration and communication and the courage to stick to your guns. The Chinese sign of the Active Wood Tiger is responsible for your sparkling personality, magnetic looks and sense of humor. The active wood element encourages you to make a success out of your own interests, but it is hard for you to work for others.

The Vedic sign of Makara brings you down to earth, as it adds common sense and a practical attitude; the Uttara Bhadra Mansion lends the ability to talk persuasively and to take on challenges with courage and fortitude. If born under the Revati Mansion, you will be a good organizer who can achieve success after a struggle, and you can expect to travel far.

The Native American Otter of the Butterfly clan ensures that you are logical, humorous and fun to be with. You make a sympathetic friend and a respected and honored boss. In West Africa, the authoritative and humanitarian Baobab Tree starts the month but soon changes to the sign of the Wealth of Amber and Silver, which gives you strong emotions and an inventive mind. This also enhances your counseling abilities.

The month starts with the Celtic tree symbol of the Cypress, which ensures good looks and a slightly aristocratic manner, but it soon changes to the Poplar, which emphasises being concerned about others. Then the dynamic Cedar comes in, adding enterprise and magnetism. In matters of love you can be oversensitive. The Runic sign of Algiz allows you to get away with things that would defeat others, but this soon changes to the headstrong sign of Sowelo, which makes it hard for you to admit to faults.

FEBRUARY ~ PISCES
19th February onward

The gentle, creative water sign of Pisces means that you love going out and meeting interesting people. You are a sucker for a hard-luck story, and you can waste years rescuing others or fulfilling their needs while neglecting your own. However, the Chinese Tiger gives you just the touch of rebellion and ambition that saves you from being a wimp. The active wood element adds to your idealism – it makes you trustworthy, and it also makes you astute and realistic.

Your Vedic sign starts out as the practical and ambitious Makara, but soon changes to the inventive and exciting sign of Kumbha, which brings a touch of much-needed obstinacy. Both these Mansions help prevent your heart from totally ruling your head. The Revati Mansion gives you organizing ability and encourages you to travel, but this soon changes to Ashwini, which makes you bold and outspoken.

The Native Americans see you as a Cougar of the Frog clan, which gives you a mystical spirit and healing ability. You can shut your feelings away when you are hurt and there is a touch of loneliness about you, but this may actually be an aid to your clairvoyant abilities. West Africans see you as belonging to the Wealth of Amber and Silver, which indicates that your emotions run deep and that you need personal space. Your understanding of human nature makes you an excellent counselor.

The Celtic Pine Tree makes you a perfectionist, and far more interested in your appearance than most Pisceans, while the Norse symbol of Sowelo gives you the ability to think and act at speed. The following Norse symbol of Tiwaz suggests strength of mind and a talent for legal argument. You keep your promises.

MARCH ~ PISCES
From the 1st to the 20th

 The water sign of Pisces signifies that your values are more spiritual than material. You are both artistic and creative, and you can live a somewhat chaotic lifestyle. The Chinese sign of the receptive wood Rabbit implies obstinacy and more of a temper than a February Piscean has, but it also makes you refined, tasteful and gives you a talent for counseling others.

The Vedic sign of Kumbha is in operation at this time, and this gives you an original and inventive turn of mind plus a friendly and humanitarian nature. The Vedic Mansion of Ashwini rules the start of this period, endowing you with a somewhat adventurous spirt and a tendency to be outspoken. This soon changes to the Bharani Mansion, which lends artistic talent – this can lead to honor, but you must beware of losses.

The Native American sign of the Cougar ensures that you are entirely comfortable with the spiritual world, but it can make it difficult for you to express your feelings and to express affection to those whom you love. The West African sign of the Wealth of Amber and Silver gives you an inventive mind and a need for freedom, but this changes to the Family, which warms your personality and encourages you to look after your community.

The Celtic Willow Tree sign indicates a strong sixth sense and an interest in dreams, spells and mysteries. This changes to the Lime Tree, which also endows spirituality and mystery but which makes you something of a perfectionist. The Norse Runic sign of Tiwaz gives you strength and the ability to keep promises, while Berkana is especially associated with motherhood and a happy home life.

March ~ Aries
From the 21st onward

The active, energetic fire sign of Aries suggests that you can rush in head first where angels fear to tread. You are honest, humorous and kind, but you can be so focused on your goals that you walk over others while achieving them. The Chinese sign is the Rabbit, which gives a touch of class and a need for close personal relationships; the receptive wood element can involve you in causes.

The original, eccentric and slightly obstinate nature of the Vedic sign of Kumba is in residence at the start of your sign, but this soon gives way to the gentle sign of Meena, which brings a mystical and spiritual element into your nature. The first of your Vedic Mansions is Bharani, signifying talent, but arguments and lawsuits may plague you. This is quickly followed by Krittika, which brings success, respect and fame, but can put you in the line of fire where politics are concerned.

The Native American sign of the Red Hawk gives you energy, and it makes you a dangerous person to fall out with. Your farsightedness enables you to make a success of an idea. The West African sign of the Family adds idealism, and a need to look after the wider community and to teach and lead others.

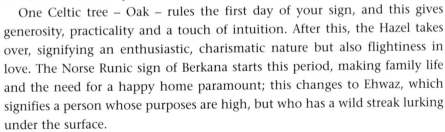

One Celtic tree – Oak – rules the first day of your sign, and this gives generosity, practicality and a touch of intuition. After this, the Hazel takes over, signifying an enthusiastic, charismatic nature but also flightiness in love. The Norse Runic sign of Berkana starts this period, making family life and the need for a happy home paramount; this changes to Ehwaz, which signifies a person whose purposes are high, but who has a wild streak lurking under the surface.

APRIL ~ ARIES
From the 1st to the 20th

The extroverted fire sign of Aries gives you great courage and optimism, and you get things done. The honest, humorous and outspoken nature of Aries is echoed by the Dragon of Chinese astrology which, being active and earth, enables you to build for the future and lead others. The Vedic sign of Meena brings a softening touch, an intuitive and spiritual element, and a strong belief system.

The first Mansion in April is Krittika, bringing success, eminence and fame – it can also be associated with political events that sometimes overtake your life. This changes to Rohini, which brings honor, intelligence, eloquence and public acclaim, after which Mrigashira takes over; this also brings honor, as a result of civil or military work.

The Native American Red Hawk of the Thunderbird clan makes you a friendly and generous person, and a strong and capable leader. This changes on the last day to the Beaver of the Turtle clan, which is slower to act and keen to improve the environment. The West African sign of the Family also encourages you to look after your community and area, but this soon changes to the sign of Small Services to the Neighborhood; people in this sign have to learn how to act with judgment on behalf of others.

The Celtic sign of the Mountain Ash makes you a little secretive at times, tough in business but kind to friends and family. The change to the Maple means increased powers of leadership and ambition, but with a soft spot for your loved ones. The Norse Runic sign of Ehwaz adds nobility, but with a hint of a wild streak beneath the surface. This changes to Mannaz, which brings a humanitarian streak and an interest in scientific or spiritual matters.

April ~ Taurus
From the 21st onward

The earth sign of Taurus makes you reliable, sensible, practical and honest. You have an artistic streak and you work well with your hands. The active earth element of your Chinese sign enhances this practicality, but also brings executive ability and a refusal to allow the grass to grow under your feet. The Chinese Dragon ensures that you are strong and stubborn, but your delightful sense of humor and kindness ensure your popularity.

The Vedic sign of Mesha adds a sprinkling of enterprise and ambition, plus the ability to lead others and to work for the betterment of others, although you would never neglect your own needs while doing so. The Mansion of Mrigashira ensures that you earn honors through working for the public or in the civil or military arena.

The Native American Beaver is known for hard work and obstinacy in the face of failure. You take your responsibilities to your family seriously and you lavish affection and attention on those you love, although you don't hesitate to argue with them when you have a point to make. The West African sign of Small Services to the Neighborhood ensures that you will have to make decisions on behalf of others. This also prevents you from jumping into anything without thinking about it first.

Your Celtic tree sign is Walnut, which makes you realistic, sensible, hardworking and courageous. You are undoubtedly a family person, and the results of your efforts in the outside world can be seen in your nice home and well cared-for family. However, you can be a little materialistic. Your Norse Runic sign is Laguz, which brings a completely different energy, being empathetic, understanding, open-minded and caring. You remain young-looking throughout your life.

May ~ Taurus
From the 1st to the 21st

 The practical earth sign of Taurus shows that you are creative, a lover of beautiful things, a family person and a reliable worker, but you would be the first to agree about your stubborn determination.

Your Chinese Snake sign denotes a reserved and private nature, with the inventive mind that is typical of the backroom worker. However, the fire element adds extroversion, enterprise and energy – in the receptive mode, this can make you a talented performer, with a great voice.

 Your Vedic sign is Mesha, which adds impulsiveness, courage, kindness, a sense of humor, but also a slightly self-centered attitude. The Mansion of Ardra brings honor and wealth through marriage, but a career with many ups and downs. Punarvasu ensures a spirited, courageous nature and keen intelligence. Sudden fame is possible, but so is a sudden loss of fortune.

The Native American sign of the industrious Beaver of the Turtle clan rules most of this period, ensuring that you take partnerships and family relationships very seriously. The West African sign of Small Services to the Neighborhood denotes the ability to be a leader in your community; later, this changes to the Market, which signifies a need for financial and emotional security due to a fluctuating pattern of work.

The first Celtic tree is the Poplar, showing that you learn and grow by experience. This changes to the Sweet Chestnut, which says that you are organized and capable, but apt to change your mind unexpectedly or do two things at once. The Norse Runic sign is gentle Laguz, which is imaginative, emotional and understanding, but later this changes to Inguz, which indicates that tradition, family life and your home will always mean a lot.

May ~ Gemini
From the 22nd onward

 The air sign of Gemini makes you gregarious, chatty, versatile and intelligent, but apt to make bad choices in relationships due to hoping that your lovers are nicer than they actually are. The Chinese Snake sign ensures that you keep important secrets to yourself while appearing outgoing and friendly. The receptive fire element gives you a touch of glamor and a love of show business, plus talent and a desire to be among exciting and talented people.

 The Vedic sign of Mesha gives those at the start of the period an impulsive and adventurous nature. The Vrishaba group is more settled and less apt to make changes just for the sake of it. The Mansion of Parnavasu ensures that you have a lively nature and keen intelligence, and it makes fame a distinct possibility. The Mansion of Pushya denotes a caring and loving nature.

The Native American Deer of the Butterfly clan makes you an excellent friend who can counsel others without judging them, but you can jump from one idea to another at the drop of a hat. The West African Market sign advises you not to get into relationships that don't offer you a future.

The Celtic tree sign of the Sweet Chestnut shows that you are very capable, but that you can switch paths rapidly and unexpectedly, while the Mountain Ash means that you have many sides to your nature – you may live a double life. The Norse Runic sign of Inguz makes family life, tradition and history important to you; for those born under the sign of Othila, property, inheritance, trade and commerce become important and valuable.

Juпe ~ Gemiпi
From the 1st to the 21st

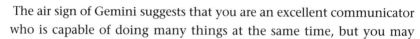

The air sign of Gemini suggests that you are an excellent communicator who is capable of doing many things at the same time, but you may suffer in relationship matters. The Chinese Horse makes you an excellent salesperson, with a love of travel and a need for freedom. This is enhanced by the active fire nature, which can lead you into a career in the military or a life of travel, change and adventure.

The Vedic sign of Vrishaba exerts a steadying influence that helps you to stick to jobs and relationships when the going gets tough. This gives you the ability to work with your hands as well as with your intellect. The Vedic Mansion of Pushya suggests a caring and loving side to your nature, which can lead you into a caring profession. This changes to Ashlesha, which is excellent for those who wish to study astrology or related subjects.

The Native American sign of Deer of the Butterfly clan makes you a tonic to those who are around you, as you can never be boring, but this changes to the home-loving Woodpecker of the Frog clan on the last day. The West African sign of the Market makes you switch between optimism and pessimism, success and sudden losses. This changes to the Ancestor, which makes you over-idealistic but able to advise others.

The first Celtic tree sign is the Ash, which reveals a many-sided personality and a tendency to rush into difficult relationships. This then changes to the Hornbeam, which endows you with charm, eloquence and a sense of responsibility. The Norse Runic sign of Othila suggests that you gain from inheritance, shrewd investments or business success. The following Norse sign of Dagaz denotes honesty and success through achievements, plus luck with money.

June ~ Cancer
From the 22nd onward

As a watery Cancerian, you love a full home life with the members of your family around or popping in and out. You are also a shrewd and cautious business person. When not working, you love to take your family traveling. The Chinese Horse sign is also a great traveler; the active fire element adds a need for adventure, which, if unfulfilled, can make you moody or hot-tempered.

The Vedic sign of Vrishaba lends an artistic streak and a talent for cooking and gardening in addition to a need for a stable life. This soon changes to the chatty and outgoing sign of Mithuna, which adds versatility and restlessness. The Vedic Mansion of Ashlesha attracts some of you to astrology and similar subjects, and it can make you an idealist. The Mansion of Magha signifies artistic talent with a touch of arrogance.

The Native American sign of the Woodpecker of the Frog clan makes you an affectionate parent who finds it hard to let the little ones go when they grow up. Woodpeckers enjoy listening to music. The West African sign of the Ancestor can lead to depression when life doesn't live up to your expectations – you may need to work at maintaining a realistic attitude.

The Celtic tree sign of the Fig ensures that you want to be the center of a large and happy family, but this soon changes to the Birch, which brings artistic talent and also common sense. The final Celtic tree is the Apple, which makes you fear change and unpredictable events. The lucky Norse Runic sign of Dagaz also adds to your idealism, giving you intuition and a desire for spiritual advancement; Fehu brings prosperity.

July ~ Cancer
From the 1st to the 22nd

 No man or woman is an island, and that is especially true for those born under the water sign of Cancer – you need to have your loved ones around you. Your shrewd common sense and caution make you an excellent business person. The Chinese sign of the Goat makes you intuitive, creative and hardworking, and the receptive earth element can bring success and leadership in business or the arts.

The Vedic sign of Mithuna gives you excellent communication ability and a touch of magic when dealing with the public, but it can also make you slightly fickle. The Vedic Mansion of Magha makes your personality stronger and more outgoing than it otherwise might be; the sexy Purva Phagune Mansion can lead to self-indulgence.

The Native American Woodpecker of the Frog clan can make you a little too dependent upon your partner and desperate for financial and emotional security. This changes to the glamorous Salmon of the Thunderbird clan before long. Fate can throw those born under the West African sign of the Ancestor into positions of leadership; when the sign changes to the Judge, this quality is enhanced, along with willpower.

Your Celtic tree signs start with the Apple, which adds grace and style but can make you worry about small matters. This changes to the Fir, which indicates a stronger, more ambitious personality, but the vulnerability is still there under the surface. The final Celtic tree sign is the Elm, which indicates a certain naïve candor. The Norse Runic sign of Fehu brings prosperity and luck, allied to a generous nature; those under the sign of Uruz have a passionate and somewhat wild side to their nature.

July ~ Leo
From the 23rd onward

The cheerful, outgoing fire sign of Leo is in evidence at this time, giving you ambition and a longing for the good things of life, but also generosity, kindness and a glorious sense of humor. Your greatest love is reserved for your children. The Chinese sign of the receptive earth Goat lends an artistic eye and the ability to work very hard indeed. The earth element makes for efficiency and a scientific turn of mind, and also a love of animals.

The Vedic sign of Mithuna endows you with excellent communication skills and a flirtatious manner, although this eventually changes to Karkarta, which signifies the classic homemaker and family person. The first Mansion for your sign is Purva Phagune, which indicates sexuality and a touch of self-indulgence, but this changes to Uttara Phalguni, which signifies a quick mind and a generous nature but sometimes a bad choice of friends.

The Native American sign of the Salmon of the Thunderbird clan lends the ability to get to the heart of any matter. You make powerful friends but also powerful enemies, despite your well-meaning and generous nature. The West African sign of the Judge denotes decisiveness, enthusiasm and energy, but it can lead to boastfulness if you are not careful.

The first Celtic tree sign in the sequence is the stately Elm, which can make you appear abrupt and brusque when all you are doing is protecting your own tender feelings. This soon changes to the Cypress, which puts you where the action is. A show business career would be indicated for some. The Norse Runic sign of Uruz means that you are constantly involved in outrageous adventures. This changes on the last day to the powerful sign of Thurisaz.

August ~ Leo
From the 1st to the 23rd

The passionate and fiery sign of Leo is in evidence now, so generosity, humor and kindness rule along with great love for your children and pets. You are easily irritated by fools or by those who seek to get in your way. The Chinese sign of the Monkey gives you an inventive mind and great commercial ability, while the active metal element makes you difficult to persuade or influence.

The Vedic sign of Karkarta adds a softening layer of intuition and sensitivity, and it also makes it imperative that you have a home you can come back to. The Vedic Mansion of Uttara Phalguni suggests a quick mind, a generous nature and the chance to achieve high honor. This changes to the Mansion of Hasta, which indicates charm and a successful life, although you can suddenly fall out of favor.

The Native American sign of the Salmon of the Thunderbird clan gives you a slightly regal air – but it hides a sensitive nature. At the end of this period, this changes to the Brown Bear of the Turtle clan, which indicates a cool exterior but a soft heart. The West African sign of the Judge begins this period, denoting a strong will and the ability to learn from experience. This soon changes to the clairvoyant and sensitive sign of the Kola Nut.

The Celtic tree signs open with the Cypress, which needs to be appreciated for what it is, but this soon changes to the Poplar, which indicates that you vacillate between fulfilling your own needs and those of others. The final Celtic tree, Cedar, belongs to a bubbly, enterprising personality. The Norse Runic signs are the strong Thurisaz, which endows leadership and ability, and then Ansuz whose influence gives a deep yearning for eternal values.

August ~ Virgo
From the 24th onward

The practical and intellectual earth sign of Virgo denotes literary and communication skills, a talent for research and an eye for detail, but with the perfectionist's tendency to worry over insignificant details. The Chinese sign of the active metal Monkey adds independence, strength, common sense, commercial ability and a talent for getting jobs done. There are times when you may work far too hard for your own good.

The Vedic sign of Karkarta signifies a cautious nature with an eye for business and a need for a strong home and family life. This changes to Simha, which indicates creativity in art and business, and the ability to make a happy home. Simha can also add a touch of arrogance or pomposity to your nature. The Vedic Mansion of Chitra brings success which can lead to wealth, plus a deep love of science and the arts.

The Native American sign of the Brown Bear of the Turtle clan gives you a cheerful nature and an excellent sense of humor, and it makes you keen to discover as much as possible about everything. The only real drawback is a tendency to take on lame ducks or try to rescue those who are beyond help. The West African sign of the Kola Nut indicates a desire to make changes just for the sake of changing, but this sign also endows you with intuition, which helps with decision making.

The Celtic tree is the Pine, which makes you reserved, introverted, modest and quiet, but still a little more egotistical than others realize. You are also more sensitive than you let on. The Norse Runic sign of Ansuz adds eloquence and a spiritual outlook; Raidho reveals a character with a noble spirit, a seeker after truth.

September ~ Virgo

From the 1st to the 22nd

The earth sign of Virgo signifies a quick mind and a talent for research and analysis, but it can make you too concerned with details. Your Chinese astrology receptive metal element adds ambition and an innovative mind, and it draws you toward the world of show business and the arts. The sign of the Rooster adds even more glamor, plus honesty, but it also means you have a tendency to brag about your achievements.

Your Vedic sign is Simha, which is noted for generosity and a love of children and family life. The first Vedic Mansion is Chitra, which can lead to success and an interest in the arts and sciences. This soon changes to Swati, which brings renown in the arts and a determined nature. The last Mansion is sociable Vashaka, which indicates good powers of concentration.

Your Native American Brown Bear of the Turtle clan signifies intelligence, curiosity, a realistic attitude and a sense of humor. The West African sign of the Kola Nut can make you changeable, but it also brings intuition, which helps you to make wise decisions. This changes to the Traveler, which can indicate physical travel or the ability to move between the real world and the spiritual world.

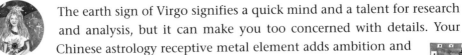

The first Celtic tree sign is Pine, which indicates passionate feelings that are hidden within your reserved outer nature. This is followed by the Willow, which signifies intuition and a love of anything mysterious. The final Celtic tree sign is the Lime, which denotes ambition and great organizing skills on the outside and a soft heart within. The Norse Runic sign is Raidho, which suggests a traveler who gains wisdom along the way. It then changes to Kaunaz, which is the sign of the inventor.